Portraits of Himalayan Flowers

PORTRAITS *of* HIMALAYAN FLOWERS

Toshio Yoshida

With a Foreword by
Daniel J. Hinkley

TIMBER PRESS
Portland · Cambridge

Frontispiece
Meconopsis horridula Hook. f. & Thoms., Papaveraceae
22 July 1989, S of Nanga La, Khumbu, alt. 5050 m, E Nepal

Page 8
Saussurea gossipiphora D. Don, Compositae
29 July 1989, Kalapattar, Khumbu, alt. 5400 m, E Nepal

First published in Japanese by Heibonsha Limited, Publishers, Tokyo, in 1994.

Published in 2002 by

Timber Press, Inc.
The Haseltine Building
133 S.W. Second Avenue, Suite 450
Portland, Oregon 97204, U.S.A.

Timber Press
2 Station Road
Swavesey
Cambridge CB4 5QJ, U.K.

Printed in Hong Kong

Library of Congress Cataloging-in-Publication Data

Yoshida, Toshio, 1949–
    [Hana no Himaraya. English]
    Portraits of Himalayan flowers / Toshio Yoshida ; with a foreword by
Daniel J. Hinkley.
       p. cm.
    Includes bibliographical references (p.).
    ISBN 0-88192-551-9
    1. Wild flowers—Himalaya Mountains. 2. Wild flowers—Himalaya
Mountains —Pictorial works. I. Title.
QK379.5.H55 Y6713 2002
582.13'095496—dc21

                       2002020458

Contents

Foreword

The recompense of observing plants in their natural habitats has little to do with botany or horticulture. In reality, the reward is that of embracing a communion with, and a celebration of, a perfected totality. Those who have ventured to desolate places to observe their floras and have not opened their hearts to the awesome weave of life through geology, climate, and culture have returned without the treasures that are afforded in every step of every passing moment.

The mystical Himalaya, with its youthful, inaccessible mountain ranges of commanding peaks and serene valleys, has long attracted the adventurer as well as the botanist. Few who have traveled here, with or without deliberate intent to study its floristic inventory, have come away untouched by the mysterious botanical creations that inhabit these high places. Whether hiking amidst majestic forests of rhododendrons or encountering the highly specialized, bizarrely configured life forms of alpine altitudes, it is not difficult to believe that one has stumbled into the enchanted landscape of Tolkien's Middle Earth.

I can recall with crystalline clarity my first encounter with the Tibetan rhubarb, *Rheum nobile*, in 1995. At 16,000 feet on Jaljale Himal in eastern Nepal, my trekking companions and I made our way up a steep and rocky pass through a soupy fog that we came to expect would envelop us each day. As we neared the summit, we observed a most incongruous assemblage of figures on the opposite shore of a small lake, or *pokari*, as it is called in Nepalese. Through the shrouded atmosphere, these pyramidal forms appeared like a band of curiously clad people that were standing in meditative stillness. Soon enough, we realized we had at last come upon the near-mythical denizens of the lofty alpine slopes of this region, and marveled at their surreal design so necessary to persevere in such an inhospitable environment. My short breath of magical befuddlement will be forever bound to my consciousness.

It is precisely this enigmatic quality of the plants and environs of the Himalaya that Toshio Yoshida captures in this book. In these photos is an understanding of the complete experience that is often too elusive to be successfully captured by film; the clangor of yak bells through blue-gray fog, the singing of Sherpas, and the whipping froth of unforgiving, relentless wind. With this seasoning of perceived sound and movement, the portraits themselves take on that inexplicable empathy of simply being there.

Simply "being there" with a camera to seize these moments, however, is not quite as elementary as it may seem. Every year innumerable outlanders trek these high places, yet the majority travel in late autumn well after the monsoon has suspended its lavish and relentless assault. The skies are then clear and offer godlike views of glacier-clad peaks in every direction. Yet frost has already drawn the flora of these hills safely down deep to their roots by this time, leaving only skeletal remains of the dreamlike colors that earlier battled the blasts of sleet and wind in this vaporous air. So simply braving the elements at the zenith of blossom, to experience the electrical pulse of *Meconopsis* or the comical, insulated propositions of *Saussurea*, is proof of the author's commitment to his craft.

Through this book, Toshio Yoshida brings to the outside world a glimpse of the almost supernatural beauty of a mostly inaccessible region—brought to us through a laborious, and undoubtedly at times uncomfortable, process. Yet there exists in these portraits no discernible trace of hardship or difficulty. Here there is only visible a highly spiritual, multidimensional intercourse with the marvelous adaptations of life and all of its associated mysteries. For these treasures, I am profoundly thankful.

DANIEL J. HINKLEY

A History of the Study of Himalayan Plants

The range of snow-covered peaks forming the Himalayas, the roof of the world, teems with life for a short time in summer. The inhabitants of the region have for countless ages used the herbs and trees that cover the crags and valleys. Plants that are not useful to them, even as forage, are regarded as weeds, however. The Himalayan flora is undoubtedly valued by these people, but modern botanical research only came about through visitors from outside the region. I would like to introduce briefly the progression of that research.

In 1600, the British established the East India Company. They considered the Himalayan region a part of India during their rule. The deep ties between the Indians and the English are pertinent to the onset and development of plant research there, as the first person to collect Himalayan plants was Francis Buchanan Hamilton, head of the British mission that visited Nepal from 1802 to 1803. It was another twenty years, however, before Nathaniel Wallich, a man who was to make a lasting contribution to Himalayan plant research, visited Nepal.

Nathaniel Wallich was born in 1786. By 1807, he was affiliated with the East India Company as a surgeon. From 1817 to 1846, he was the director of the company's botanic gardens on the outskirts of Calcutta. This garden would later become the Royal Botanic Garden, Calcutta (today the Indian Botanic Garden), and has served a major role in the study of the flora of India. Wallich collected plants from each region of India and was in Nepal from 1820 to 1822. The area he surveyed for the most part is Gosainkund (about 4200 m elevation), which is north of Kathmandu. In 1825, David Don wrote the first book on Nepalese flora, *Prodromus Florae Napalensis,* which was based on the plants Wallich collected, as well as on Hamilton's specimens.

Wallich himself published *Tentamen Florae Napalensis Illustratae* between 1824 and 1826. Consisting of 50 plant illustrations, it became the first illustrated publication of Nepalese plants. Between 1828 and 1849, Wallich published *A Numerical List of the Dried Specimens,* a mimeographed list from the Calcutta garden; it was the first comprehensive list of Indian and Himalayan plants. Many botanical names in this list have the author's name "Wall." (for Wallich), but Wallich did not formally publish the names of the plants himself. This has lead to continued confusion regarding the scientific names of many Indo-Himalayan plants.

Another monumental, early illustrated book on Himalayan plants is *Illustrations of the Botany and Other Branches of the Natural History of the Himalayan Mountains, and of the Flora of Cashmere* (1833–1840) by John Forbes Royle. Born in 1800, Royle became curator of the garden at Saharanpur, Uttar Pradesh, in 1833. During his residence at Mussoorie, he mainly researched the flora of Kashmir. His massive 472-page flora included 97 pages of botanical plates done mostly by the famous Indian botanical illustrator Vishnuprasaud. Some plates are by others, including the exceptional J. D. C. Sowerby and C. M. Curtis. Royle published many new plants in this book, so the text is also valuable from a scientific point of view. The notes on the new plants, however, are simple and occasionally inaccurate.

Equal in importance to these illustrated flora are the explorers' journals and travel records that raised the curiosity of so many eager readers. The well-known Victor Jacquemont, friend of the writer Stendahl, published his four-volume *Voyage dans l'Inde* from 1841 to 1844. The fourth volume described the flora and fauna of India. A separate volume named *Atlas* illustrated the plants he collected. Jacquemont himself did not study the plants but instead turned them over to botanists Joseph Decaisne and Jacques Cambessèdes.

The western Himalayas that Royle and Jacquemont surveyed is arid with little summer rain. For variety of plant life, it is inferior to the eastern Himalayas, but it was ideal for summer vacationing. For that reason, it was developed as a resort area and the plants growing there became more familiar to European visitors.

The research in Indian flora that began with Wallich at Calcutta continued with great vigor. Joseph Dalton Hooker, a friend of the evolutionist Charles Darwin, first set foot in the Himalayas in 1848. He entered the famous tea region of Darjeeling and advanced to Sikkim-Himalaya. The itinerary of his travels was published in 1854 as *Himalayan Journals,* which is famous as the first account of travel in the Himalayas. Hooker pushed on toward the upper alpine areas and was the first outsider to explore plants of the eastern Himalayas. He was fascinated not only by the perennials but by the numerous rhododendrons there. From this point, his research turned exclusively to Himalayan plants. Among his major accomplishments is the seven-volume *The Flora of British India* (1872–1897) which he wrote and edited. This work established a new level of research in Himalayan flora. It is still useful to botanists today. Hooker also had an artistic side and made numerous sketches during his travels. *The Rhododendrons of Sikkim-Himalaya* (1849–1851) and *Illustrations of Himalayan Plants* (1855) are among the publications based on his sketches which are considered some of the finest classic botanical drawings ever (not simply of the Himalayan plants).

More than a few Himalayan plants are suitable for the British climate. As the art of hybridizing advanced and growers became able to cross these new plants with traditional plants, the value of Himalayan plants as hybrid parents increased. Nurseries schemed to send seed collectors to the Himalayas. Both the Kew and the Edinburgh botanical gardens had collected plant specimens from the Himalayas, which for the most part have been underused effectively until recently.

As of 2001, the easiest Himalayan country to visit is Nepal, but a survey of its plants was very late coming into being. Until the 1950s, Nepal remained an isolated country, closed to foreigners for the purpose of scientific research. During that period, no Nepalese conducted research. The British were the first to study Nepalese plants when the country was opened in the 1950s. They were followed by the Japanese.

Adam Stainton (1921–1991) was a banker and plant lover. Not only did he participate in the field exploration of plants, but he also provided financial support and organization for a survey of the Nepalese flora. A book of his photographs, *Flowers of the Himalayas* (1984), and its *Supplement* (1988), brought a modern sensibility to presenting the diversity of Himalayan plants to plant lovers throughout the world.

In the 1950s, after Japan began to recover from the effects of World War II, the number of Japanese who desired to go overseas for scholarly research and mountain climbing increased. Many expedition teams were dispatched. There had been speculation that the plants of Japan and those of the Himalayas have common ancestors. Professor Hiroshi Hara of the University of Tokyo conducted a comprehensive study to prove this in the 1960s. A survey team composed entirely of botanists was dispatched to Sikkim, Nepal, and Bhutan. They joined forces with a British team to compile a three-volume work, *An Enumeration of the Flowering Plants of Nepal* (1978–1982). This work is a joint project of the British Natural History Museum and the University of Tokyo.

My colleagues and I have been able to tackle new areas of plant research thanks to the work of Professor Hara. One of the problems that the team has investigated is the origin and development of special adaptations of alpine plants.

I happened to meet Toshio Yoshida in Kathmandu in the summer of 1985 while doing research. He requested my help in identifying the plants in his photographs. Since that time I have met him on many occasions and made suggestions on how to identify plants and consult available references. He has become a true student of Himalayan botany.

Mr. Yoshida takes detailed photographs to reveal the special adaptations of the various species he studies. Of course, that is not all he does, but that is what distinguishes his work, in my opinion. By getting up close to actual plants, he has been able to give us information about them photographically that no one has been able to do so. His photos give you the illusion of actually being present on the spot in the Himalayas. I hope that you will enjoy this leisurely stroll up in the land of the clouds.

HIDEAKI OHBA
Professor of Botany
University Museum, University of Tokyo

Acknowledgments

First, I would like to thank Professor Hideaki Ohba, plant taxonomist at the University of Tokyo, who kindly wrote the foreword to the Japanese edition of this book. From the start, he has advised me on the Himalayan plants included in this publication. While gathering illustrations for this book, I asked him to review each photo, and in the process learned many things about the plants. The explanatory texts beneath each photo are based on the field notes of my observations and impressions at the time I took the photos. These are different from taxonomical notes reflecting the variability of each species.

Concerning the preparation of this English edition, I owe a special debt of gratitude to David G. Long of the Royal Botanic Garden, Edinburgh, for providing me with new information on Himalayan plants, not only in *Flora of Bhutan* of which he is the main author, but also in a letter in which he responded to my queries about plant names. Dr. Long cooperated with other colleagues, including Dr. L. S. Springate, who settled several uncertain identifications of Compositae.

I also thank the many botanists of Tokyo's Society of Himalayan Botany who assisted me with research during their regular meetings. In particular, Masayuki Mikage of Kanazawa University answered my inquires about the anatomy of *Ephedra*, and Hiroshi Ikeda of Okayama University of Science gave me several taxonomic suggestions on *Potentilla*.

The excellent layout of every page is the work of Sei-ichi Tagawa, an experienced editorial designer with deep interest in Himalaya where he has trekked several times.

I also thank Maurice Horn, an American plant enthusiast and fluent Japanese speaker who thoroughly reviewed the translation of this book. Another American nurseryman, Dan Hinkley, also reviewed the text and wrote a foreword to the English-language edition.

Finally, I with to express my deepest gratitude to all the staff members of my personal expeditions during the worst seasons for trekking in Himalaya. These guides, organizers, cooks, kitchen boys, and porters were drawn from Nepal, India, Sikkim, Bhutan, Tibet, and Pakistan. Despite their routine of hard work, they never hesitated to reach out to help me up steep slopes, across rivers, and through deep snow.

Introduction

In October 1984, I woke up with a headache from altitude sickness in a small village north of the Annapurna Massif. Exiting the hut in which I had spent the night, I passed through a narrow doorway into a barren field shrouded in bright morning mist. A voice chanting a strange melody drew me out. In the field, a herd of male yaks and some scattered stones stood among the reddish stubble of just-harvested buckwheat. The yaks turned their heads toward me. These massive animals had transported a load from a distant pasture and were still breathing heavily, their breaths visible in the air. They trembled nervously. Beyond the field, an old man collected dried yak dung.

Foreigners sometimes think of the Himalayas as rising steeply from their bases to their peaks; on the contrary, gentle slopes often spread out like waves around rocky hills that were carved by glacial movement. In summer, these slopes are mainly used as pasture for yaks. Alpine plants flourish there thanks to a combination of sunrays shining above the thick layers of clouds that enshroud the lower slopes and cool moisture borne on upward drafts of air rising from the south. Herds of female yaks graze the tender grasses of the broad slopes during the day and are returned to their milking sites toward evening. During the night they drop their nutrient-rich dung which is used for both fertilizer and fuel. In the dry areas where woody material is scarce, yak dung is a treasured fuel source.

As the old man collected dung, he recited a mantra, synchronizing his movements with his words. He breathed in the traditional way of highlanders. The mantra, from Tibetan Buddhism, is generally intoned, "Om Mani Padme Hum." "Om" is one of the ways to address God. "Mani" means "jewel," "precious treasure," or "Buddhist law." "Padme" means "inside the lotus flower," and "Hum" is an exclamatory word used to complete the rhythm of the mantra. The old man prolonged the sound of the "Om" and sped through the "jewel inside the lotus."

Although the lotus is a subtropical plant and does not grow in alpine regions, it has been associated with the Himalayas. From antiquity, Indians have considered the snowy peaks of the Himalayas to be the residence of the gods and have compared them to the flower of the lotus, *Nelumbo nucifera.* The Buddha Shakyamuni symbolized his teachings as the pure lotus flower rising from dirty pond water. Hindus in the Garhwal-Himalaya and Buddhists in the Bhutan-Himalaya make offerings of the flowering stems of *Saussurea obvallata*, peeling back the white bracts till they resemble lotus flowers (see page 109). Furthermore, the Chinese name for some *Saussurea* species is *Xue Lian Hua* or "snowy lotus flower."

When the old man had filled the bamboo basket on his back with dried dung, he stepped into the dark hut and sat cross-legged beside a hearth. Placing some of the collected dung between pieces of a shrubby juniper, he made a fire and prepared a pot of butter-tea, which he shared with me. Then, he drew a long rosary out of his breast pocket. The rosary had 108 beads made of the seeds of holy fig, *Ficus indica.* Holding the rosary with both hands in his lap, the old man resumed murmuring the mantra while swaying his upper body back and forth. With each recitation, he moved one bead on his rosary to the side. The mantra sank deep into my subconscious as I stayed in the hut to recover. In fact, since hearing the old man recite "Om Mani Padme Hum" beside his fire, it has become my habit to chant these words whenever I am troubled or have difficulty catching my breath while climbing.

Like the old man who sought spiritual treasure in his mantra, I, too, was looking for a precious treasure in the Himalayas, though of a more physical kind. Two years later, in August 1986, I entered an uninhabited glacial valley with a Sherpa guide and some porters. It was my first experience trekking in the upper alpine zone above 5000 m elevation during the summer monsoon period.

For the four months of summer, from June to September, monsoon rains attack this region from

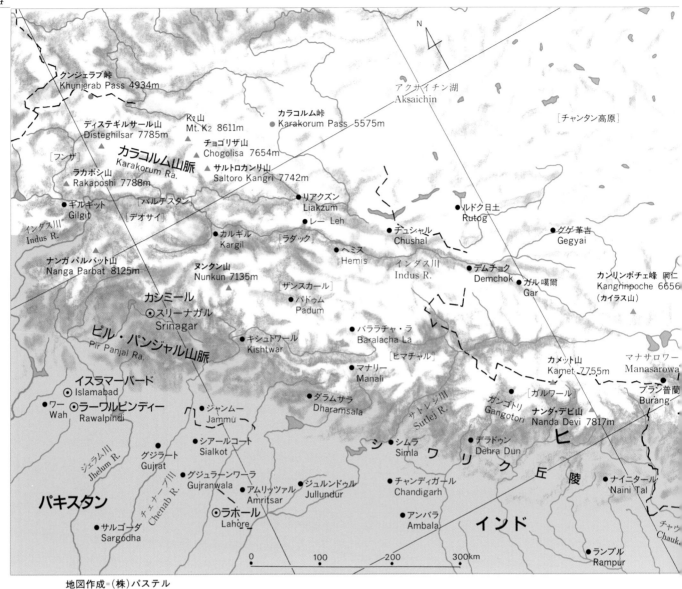

地図作成=(株)パステル

the Indian Ocean to the south. The monsoon tends to be shorter in the western region and longer in the eastern region. During this period, roads running along the steep slopes of the mountainside are frequently washed out from place to place. Even small streams, which are easy to straddle in the dry season, turn into hazardous torrents of mud and rock continuing for days in the worst cases. There are also dreadful leeches, elastic as rubber bands, which swarm out to take hold of any warm-blooded creature they can find.

Alpine slopes in midsummer are shrouded almost every day in mists that blow up from the glacial valleys. Intermittent rain or sleet accompanies them. There are few trekkers at this time of year in the upper alpine regions because they would almost never catch sight of the snowy peaks

even if they managed to endure the dangers and discomfort. It is too early for climbers to set up base camps for post-monsoon climbing. August is also too early for villagers to harvest the hay that will feed their cattle in the winter. The summer monsoons, however, mark the height of activity for the plants and animals of the alpine region.

The Khumbu glacial valley where I found myself was hardly forlorn. A herd of male yaks left behind here in the highest pasture was grazing contentedly. A flock of Tibetan snow cocks in the scree beside the path suddenly called out a warning at the sight of us intruders. Their calls sounded like human laughter. A Himalayan mouse-hare was coming and going through a hole in the stone wall of a locked mountain hut. A group of red-billed choughs was playing in the strong updraft above,

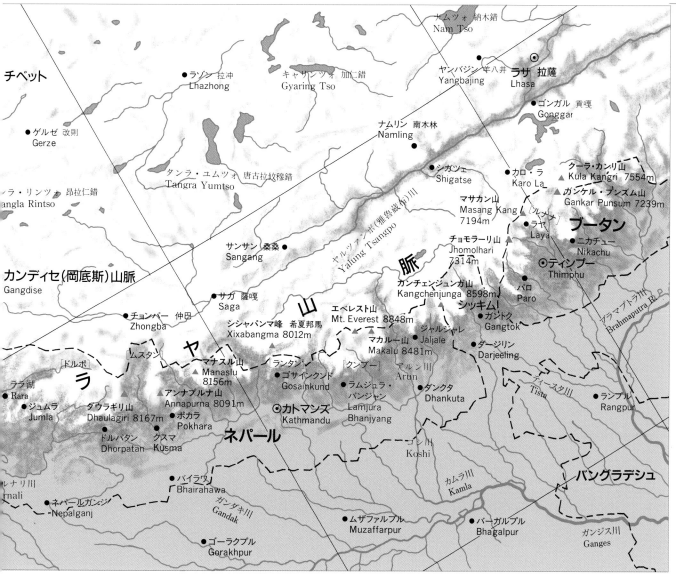

and alpine accentors and other migrating birds were moving about actively on the misty rocks and grasslands.

Next to the glacier was a long, narrow moraine. Between the moraine and the mountain slope was a narrow valley with a small stream running through it. As we moved upstream along the glacier, we came across many plants with relatively large, showy flowers on short stems, one of the characteristics of alpine flora. These included solitary flowerheads with longish, pink ray florets of an aster blooming in the white gravel; ivory flowers of a saxifrage colorfully patterned with fine spotting; tiny purple gentians opening directly on the ground surrounded by elaborate rosette leaves; tufted plants of a dwarf edelweiss glittering with golden woolly hairs; and blue poppies with intensely colored,

miniature flowers so different from the large blue flowers blooming in the shadows of the cliffs lower down. All these flowers looked like large jewels scattered over the bleak highlands by the hand of God and left there because no one had dared to touch them. Chanting "Om Mani Padme Hum" in the mountain air, I was elated, even as my head ached and I gasped for air. I had found the jewel in the lotus at last.

Then I climbed Kalapattar, a hill known for its viewpoint of Mt. Everest. As luck would have it, the mists parted and Mt. Everest, shrouded in white snow, was suddenly revealed over the Khumbu Glacier. The stony ground was warmed by the fierce and sudden sunlight of high summer.

From out of nowhere Apollo butterflies appeared one by one and gathered on a stony hillside, busily visiting the alpine flowers and beginning their territorial competition in mid-air. Large bumblebees entered the cottonball-like *Saussurea gossipiphora* and emerged a bit later covered with yellow pollen. A swarm of rove beetles, sheltered in the partially closed flowers of a blue poppy, resumed its movements. The drab stony hill became animated by lively activity.

No sooner had the chilly mists begun to rise again, clouding over the sun, than the tiny gentians immediately closed their mouths of purple flowers. The Apollo butterflies held fast to small white pebbles that mimicked their wing color and ceased to flutter. Almost all the bumblebees fled somewhere else, but two or three stragglers clung to the outside of the cottonballs, frozen into inactivity.

These dwarf upper alpine plants developed their disproportionately large and brightly colored flowers not to attract human eyes, of course, but to draw distant pollinators to them as soon as there is clear weather. The fact that we humans are so strongly impressed when we see these flowers perhaps is due to a sensibility that runs through all living creatures. From this point forward, I began to view flowers through the eyes of pollinators.

This book contains 108 photographs (one each for the beads in a Tibetan rosary); these are the fruits of ten years of research in Bhutan, Sikkim, Nepal, northern India, Kashmir, Pakistan, and southern Tibet. With the exception of the Assam-Himalaya, these are roughly all of the regions of the Himalayas.

The photographs are arranged in taxonomic order, by family, so readers can identify similarities between species and genera. Some photographs in this book, for example, *Rheum nobile* on page 17 (facing), were taken in the mists under an umbrella. For the most part, however, I waited until the sky cleared to snap the shutter. Looking at these pictures, you might imagine that the Himalayan summer is a world filled with light blue skies and snowy peaks set against fluffy clouds. In truth, it is not rare to camp for long periods in a corner of a valley that is soaked with cold rain every day—blue sky, or even an outline of the sun, might not appear for up to two weeks.

Further, for the most part, I took the photos right up close to the subject plants. As a result, the flowers appear larger than they would to a person standing nearby or bending over. The sizes of the saxifrages on pages 42 and 44 are much larger than the actual flowers. To see these flowers on a large scale, I had to become like a pollinator, sitting or laying on the ground, not worrying about getting my hands or clothes dirty, and bringing my face right up to the flower.

Rheum nobile Hook. f. & Thoms.   Polygonaceae

This rhubarb relative grows on rocky slopes in the upper alpine zone where it is exposed to endless, cold summer rain and sleet. Inside a raincoat of pale yellow bracts, the daytime temperature is at least five degrees (Celsius) warmer than the outside air, and small yellow-green flowers rise up in dense clusters 5–10 cm tall. The plant reaches 40–100 cm tall at flowering time and up to 2 m when the fruits mature. After the bracts turn brown in late autumn, they shrivel up, allowing wind to blow off the buckwheat-like fruits. The snowball-like plant on the right is *Saussurea gossipiphora*. 10 July 1990, N of Jaljale Himal, alt. 4500 m, E Nepal

Bistorta macrophylla (D. Don) Soják Polygonaceae

Completely covering alpine grassland grazed by yaks and sheep, this bistort is unusual for its brilliant color, which would be welcome in any flower garden. The rootstock is buried more than 5 cm deep. Despite being trampled on and nibbled by immense yaks and being continuously exposed to the dry winter weather, the plant can sprout stems again the following year. The tiny pink flowers droop to quickly drain dew and rain, and are densely clustered on inflorescences 1–3 cm long. The plant can be 5–20 cm tall. The bamboolike, dark green leaves are 5–10 cm long and 1–2 cm wide. The lengthwise striations were formed while the leaf was still in bud and look like parallel veins after

the leaves have opened. The yellow flowers dotting the photo are *Saxifraga aristulata*. In the lower center is a tuft of yellowish-green woolly-leaved *Anaphalis xylorhiza*. On both sides toward the back are dwarf *Rhododendron nivale*. Hairy pinnate leaves in the lower right belong to a pea relative, *Spongiocarpella purpurea*. The glacial lake Barun Pokhari and the icefall from Mt. Makalu form the distant backdrop. 28 July 1990, S of Mt. Makalu, alt. 4800 m, E Nepal

Bistorta vacciniifolia (Wall. ex Meisner) Greene   Polygonaceae

At the end of summer, these flowers suddenly rise on countless up-right stems 5–15 cm tall, carpeting massive rocky outcrops like red flames. The tough woody stems are well branched and form large colonies. Each colony is composed of one plant, which can spread to 2 m in diameter. Leaves are ovate to elliptic and 1–2 cm long. Red leaf stipules surround the flowering stems. The terminal spikelike clusters are 2–4 cm long. Mt. Langtang Lirung (7245 m) can be seen in the background covered with fresh snow. 5 September 1991, right bank of Lirung Glacier, Langtang Himal, alt. 4250 m, C Nepal

Aconogonon tortuosum (D. Don) Hara   Polygonaceae

This perennial grows in northern valleys surrounded by high peaks which do not receive much moisture from the monsoons. It usually forms a rounded shrublike plant 30–50 cm tall with the well-divided stems that characterize plants of dry, windy regions. The ovate to elliptical leaves are 2–4 cm long, twisted, and covered with minute hairs. The spikelike terminal inflorescence is 1–3 cm long with cream-colored flowers 4 mm in diameter. Although the reddish stems and green leaves are pliant, yaks and goats do not graze any part of the plant. The pyramidal ridge of Toshain Peak (6325 m) can be seen in the background. 31 July 1993, E of Mt. Nanga Parbat, alt. 4000 m, N Pakistan

Silene nigrescens (Edgew.) Majumdar   Caryophyllaceae

This campion, growing on gravelly moraines at the foot of glaciers, experiences cold rain, dry wind, and strong sunshine in the upper alpine zone. The balloonlike calyx, which attracts pollinators and protects reproductive organs, expands until the fruit has developed enough to protrude from it. The 7- to 20-cm-long stems bear solitary pendent flowers at their tips. The narrow basal foliage is opposite and 2–4 cm long. Red-stained petals protrude from the calyx and recurve. Elliptic leaves in the lower center are *Rhododendron anthopogon*. In the background, a glacier proceeds from Mt. Bhundang Ri (6150 m). 22 August 1991, upper Langtang Valley, alt. 4600 m, C Nepal

Caltha scaposa Hook. f. & Thoms.   Ranunculaceae

This dwarf relative of marsh marigold (*Caltha palustris*) was able to colonize this moist grassland after the snow melted, presumably not long ago, and grazing yaks and sheep conveniently weeded out the competition. The basal leaves are ovate, 2.5–3.5 cm long, and deeply heart shaped at their bases. Part of the scapes and the leaf stalks is underground. The 2- to 3-cm-wide flowers have five thick petal-like orange-yellow sepals. In the right foreground is a colony of similarly yellow-flowered *Geum elatum,* a member of the rose family. Primroses and anemones also bloom nearby. 21 June 1991, N of Dhorpatan, alt. 4100 m, W Nepal

Anemone polyanthes D. Don   Ranunculaceae

Deep wine-red and pure white flowers of this variable anemone species colonize in pastures, as the photo shows, and form large solitary clumps at the edge of forests or among rocks. Silken hairs cover the fat 10- to 30-cm-tall stems, which carry clusters of 2.5- to 3-cm-wide flowers at the tip. The petal-like sepals are elliptical. The deeply cut five-lobed leaves are 3–8 cm wide and covered with long hairs on both surfaces. In the left foreground are the toothed, three-lobed leaves of *Potentilla argyrophylla* var. *atrosanguinea.* In the right foreground are the oblong-lanceolate leaves of an unidentified *Bistorta* species. 21 June 1991, N of Dhorpatan, alt. 4200 m, W Nepal

Anemone obtusiloba D. Don   Ranunculaceae

The most common anemone in Himalayan alpine pastures or forest clearings exhibits great color variation. In the eastern Himalaya, white flowers and blue-violet flowers often grow together, even on the same plant, as seen here. In the western Himalayas, flowers are yellow, a color uncommon in this genus. The flowers are 3 cm across; the leaves are deeply three-lobed and 2–4 cm wide. The small yellow flowers in the foreground of the photo belong to _Ranunculus brotherusii_. The toothed, three-lobed leaves in the foreground and the vermilion flowers in the upper half of the photo belong to _Potentilla argyrophylla_ var. _atrosanguinea_. 20 June 1991, N of Dhorpatan, alt. 3900 m, W Nepal

Delphinium brunonianum Royle   Ranunculaceae

I am awed whenever I see this large delphinium growing in the upper alpine areas where few plants can survive except lichens and some tiny perennials. At 10–25 cm tall, it is covered with crystalline hairs. Stems and leaf stalks elongate among boulders. The deeply three-lobed leaves are 5–7 cm across. The 3- to 4-cm-wide flowers have five petal-like sepals which overlap to conceal four petals, which are blackish with gold bristles. The petal bases with nectaries are inserted in the fat spur on the back of the flower. Visiting insects can suck the nectar comfortably in the warm hooded room even in bad weather. 22 August 1991, W of Pemthang Karpo, Langtang Himal, alt. 4550 m, C Nepal

Paraquilegia microphylla (Royle) J. R. Drumm. & Hutch. Ranunculaceae

To get this photograph, I had to cling to an exposed rock face for a long time until the flowers stopped swaying in the wind. The roots are set into small cracks in the rock. The countless needlelike remnants of old stems and petioles underneath the new foliage indicate these plants have been blooming here for many years. The 1- to 3-cm compound leaves are divided into three smaller lobes. The 2.5- to 4-cm-wide flowers have five rounded petal-like sepals which are generally white in wetter regions and mauve in drier areas, as seen here. The true petals are small and orange colored, and they secrete nectar. 1 July 1991, in central Dolpo, alt. 4750 m, W Nepal

Corydalis calliantha Long   Papaveraceae

(Upper photograph) Found on screes exposed to monsoons, this corydalis has yellow (insect-damaged) flowers, which at 2–2.5 cm long are
larger than those of the related *Corydalis meifolia*. The 5- to 7-cm-long
glaucous leaves are divided into segments less than 1 mm wide.
25 September 1993, upstream of Nikachu, alt. 4500 m, C Bhutan

Corydalis inopinata Prain   Papaveraceae

(Lower photograph) Only 8 cm in diameter, this corydalis had just begun to flower in a scree scoured by strong winds. The succulent three-
lobed, compound leaves are 1 cm long. The 1.5-cm-long flowers have
a narrow spur at the back that cannot be seen here. 16 August 1992,
near the top of Karo La, alt. 5000 m, S Tibet

Papaver nudicaule L.   Papaveraceae

The biennial Iceland poppy that decorates our spring flowerbeds is well distributed throughout Central Asia including the western Himalayas. In the plant's native habitat, where the rhizomes run underground, numerous spent flower stems indicate the plant is a true perennial. It reaches 15–25 cm tall. The leaves are 1.5–3 cm long and plume shaped with five to seven lobes. The 2-cm-wide flowers are yellow to burnt orange. Compared to the garden hybrids, these are clearly smaller. The entire plant is covered in rough bristles. The ovaries are covered with six to eight yellow stigmas. 20 July 1993, northern rim of Deosai Plains, alt. 4500 m, N Pakistan

Meconopsis grandis Prain · Papaveraceae

No other blue poppy species has larger flowers. In the photo, the flowers are 12 cm in diameter, but in meadows fertilized by random yak droppings, they can reach 15 cm. The color, which tends to be paler on misty slopes or in shady places among shrubs and deeper in sunny places, ranges from palest blue, rich blue, and blue violet to deep wine-red. Many garden-worthy hybrid forms are available. The plant is 30–100 cm tall and covered with golden bristles that are rough to the touch but fall off easily. The basal leaves have stalks, and the narrow blades are 10–30 cm long. The flower stems have whorled bracts. 11 July 1990, NW of Topke Gola, alt. 4550 m, E Nepal

Meconopsis sherriffii Taylor   Papaveraceae

Growing in drier regions of northern Bhutan and adjacent Tibet, this is the only *Meconopsis* species with bright pink flowers. The plant is 25–40 cm tall and densely covered with long golden hairs. The many old leaf bases at the base of stems indicate this species is a perennial. The stems have whorled bracts similar to those of *Meconopsis grandis,* but the bracts are always at the lower part of stems and without stalks. Red flowers with ovate leaves in the upper right of the photo belong to *Rhodiola crenulata,* and the pinkish-white flowers with elliptic dark-green leaves in the lower left belong to *Rhododendron anthopogon.* 30 June 1992, near Dangey, E of Lunana, alt. 4800 m, N Bhutan

Meconopsis paniculata Prain   Papaveraceae

The most common poppy in Nepal, this species is often abundant on grassy slopes exposed to monsoons, especially the shrub-covered slopes near herdsmen's camping sites that have been recently burned to encourage germination of grasses. The large plants growing among forests in lower altitude usually have numerous smaller flowers. The plant is 1–2 m tall, covered with long golden bristles and minute hairs, and has a stout, hollow stem filled by drinkable water. Because it dies after flowering, the plant never forms a clump. A snow-covered peak of Mt. Khatang (6782 m) is in the background of the photo. 20 June 1989, near Dudh Kund, Solu, alt. 3950 m, E Nepal

Meconopsis horridula Hook. f. & Thom. Papaveraceae

Growing on dry, rocky slopes at the highest elevation of any blue poppy, this species is armed with fierce spines and has flowers the color of Tibetan skies. It is normally 15–30 cm tall with a flower diameter of 4–6 cm on each leafless scape. In very windy places, it is more diminutive. It is not rare to find plants 5 cm tall with flowers 3 cm across. At lower elevations, the plant can be enlarged with a leafy stem. The narrow elliptical leaves have wavy margins. When rain or snow falls, the flowers quickly respond by partially closing. 24 July 1989, NW of Gokyo, Khumbu, alt. 5100 m, E Nepal

Meconopsis bella Prain   Papaveraceae

A final flower remains on a 10-cm-tall stem, but numerous spent flower stems reach more than double that length. Like the Japanese *Pinguicula ramosa,* the stems recurve so that the large 1.5-cm fruits can split to drop their many seeds in indentations in the same rock. The four-petalled flower is 4 cm in diameter. The 1- to 2-cm leaves are on long petioles and generally narrowly ovate; however, there are some which get larger and develop lobes. This perennial grows in cliffs and in depressions in steep grassy slopes. 27 September 1993, upstream of Nikachu, alt. 4100 m, C Bhutan

Meconopsis napaulensis DC. Papaveraceae

Reaching 2 m tall, these large blue poppies bloom in forests of junipers and rhododendrons. The pinnate leaves are 30–50 cm long and well divided. Individual sections are triangularly lance shaped and somewhat point away from the plant. Larger sections are divided again. The flowers are 6–10 cm in diameter and either purple-blue (as shown here) or dark red. The two colors never appear together. There are many crosses between this species and *Meconopsis paniculata,* and often it is difficult to tell them apart. The yellow flowers in the photo are of an unidentified potentilla. 12 July 1990, W of Topke Gola, alt. 3700 m, E Nepal

Rhodiola tibetica (Hook. f. & Thoms.) Fu   Crassulaceae

This *Sedum* relative grows on the dry stony slopes of Tibet and the western Himalayas. The well-divided rootstock is visible above ground and bears numerous dark brown dried remnants of stems. Five to ten leafy stems radiate out from each tip of the divided rootstock, forming one large plant. Leafy stems are 7–12 cm tall; leaves thick, linear-lanceolate, 7–10 mm long. The terminal dark red inflorescences are 1–2 cm in diameter. The flowers have five sepals, petals, and pistils. The plant in the photo is a female plant without stamens. 17 July 1993, northern rim of Deosai Plains, alt. 4300 m, N Pakistan

Rhodiola bupleuroides (Wall. ex Hook. f. & Thoms.) Fu   Crassulaceae

Widely seen from temperate forests to upper alpine areas, this species changes shape depending on the situation. In lower elevations, the stems grow to 70 cm long and the inflorescences open flatly around the top. Seen here is a dwarf form from rocky cliffs at upper alpine elevations. The 3- to 7-mm-long leaves are broadly ovate, alternating on the short stems. The flowers are 3–4 mm in diameter with a tendency toward parts in groups of four. Yellow flowers on the right side are *Saxifraga saginoides* surrounded by *Arenaria polytricoides*. Plants covered with white woolly hairs on the left are *Hippolytia gossypina*. 3 August 1989, E of Chukung, Khumbu, alt. 5000 m, E Nepal

Rhodiola crenulata (Hook. f. & Thoms.) H. Ohba   Crassulaceae

This large species has a wide range of distribution from central Nepal to southwestern China. It is often seen in the scree around Mt. Everest. The plant grows on stony slopes or among rocks in the upper alpine zone, often near glaciers, and usually forms rounded clumps to 50 cm across or more. Numerous leafy stems from 10 to 20 cm tall radiate from the heads of the widely branched rootstock. The plant in the photo has only male flowers, the ovary much reduced, red-colored, stamens slightly longer than petals. The thick leaves are 1.5–3 cm long and the

terminal flower clusters are 2–4 cm wide. The snow-covered ridge in the upper right of the photo appears continuous with the slope on which plants grow because of an extreme clarity of the air, but is actually separated by Barun Glacier which is one of the biggest glaciers in Nepal. Mt. Lhotse (8516 m) of Khumbu Himal glowing white can be seen in the left, the main peak of which is however concealed behind the eastern peak named Lhotse Shar. 26 July 1990, right bank of Barun Glacier, S of Mt. Makalu, alt. 4950 m, E Nepal

Christolea himalayensis (Cambess.) Jafri   Cruciferae

Known also by the synonym *Ermania himalayensis,* this species grows on bleak, unstable screes of upper alpine zone alternately freezing and melting daily, even in midsummer. It is not easy to find the slate-colored plants among similarly colored stones without the showy flowers. The 5- to 10-cm-tall plant is covered with white soft hairs and has a long woody rootstock. The stem is usually divided near the base to four to six spreading branches. The flowers are 6–8 mm across, yellow suffused with pink. This is among the highest dwelling seed plants with specimens reportedly from India's Mt. Kamet at 6400 m in altitude. 11 June 1988, N of Mt. Dhaulagiri, alt. 4700 m, C Nepal

Saxifraga pilifera Hook. f. & Thoms.　　　　　Saxifragaceae

Numerous red runners reaching 10 cm long weave out from gaps in the basal leaves. The tiny plantlets at their ends set down narrow roots in between the rocks, thus forming a securely linked community. Growing in scree in upper alpine areas, the plant usually reaches 2–3 cm tall. The leaves, which are covered in short hairs around the margin, are 5–10 cm long. The green calyces and dull reddish-brown petals are approximately the same shape and 2–3 mm long. There is a gap between each petal. The yellow-green ovary is 1 mm high and has a flattened appearance. 21 July 1989, S of Nangpa La, Khumbu, alt. 5250 m, E Nepal

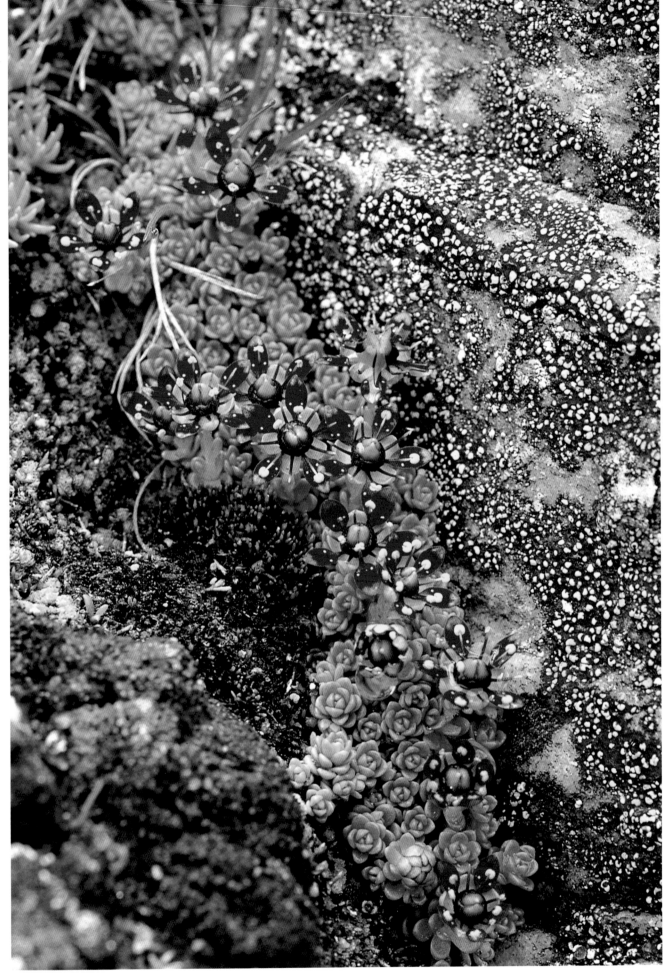

Saxifraga engleriana H. Smith   Saxifragaceae

It was a breathtaking experience to find these pretty perennials stud-
ded with exotic coral-colored flowers. The plants had formed a small
mat with branched delicate rhizomes running under the thin humus of
lichens and mosses in a shallow depression of a cliff-face at eye level.
Including the flower, this plant is only 1–3 cm tall. The fleshy leaves
are 2–4 mm long. The solitary flowers are 7–10 cm in diameter. The elliptic petals are very rarely coral colored with two yellow dots at the
base as in the photo. Usually they are yellow with many darker dots. A
dark red disk rises around the ovary. 15 July 1989, N of Gokyo, Khumbu, alt. 5100 m, E Nepal

Saxifraga pulvinaria H. Smith   Saxifragaceae

This saxifrage buries the hollows of vertical cliffs under a cushion of new rosettes that cover over the numerous old rosettes of previous years. Each 3- to 5-mm-wide rosette is smaller than one flower, which is 6 mm in diameter. The fleshy narrow leaves are 2–4 mm long. The surfaces of the leaves are encrusted so hard that moisture does not pass through them; however, a hole at the flat apex of the leaf allows sufficient moisture to be discharged to prevent the plant from freezing on evenings when the temperature falls. 9 June 1992, S of Mt. Chomolhari, alt. 4300 m, W Bhutan

Saxifraga punctulata Engl.   Saxifragaceae

Growing in level gravel to only 2–4 cm tall, the 1- to 1.5-cm-wide ivory-colored flowers look like the surrounding granite pebbles and are difficult to see with the human eye. There are two yellow spots and numerous dark red spots on each petal. The yellow spots mimic the anthers. On the north side of Mt. Kangchenjunga, the flowers become cream or deep yellow in color. On the deep yellow petals, the yellow spots become almost indistinguishable, but I wonder if they aren't clearly visible to the eyes of visiting insects. The narrow leaves are 3–7 mm long and are entirely covered in dark red glandular hairs. 29 July 1989, at Gorakshep, Khumbu, alt. 5200 m, E Nepal

Saxifraga saginoides Hook. f. & Thoms.　　　　Saxifragaceae

This species is common on moraine slopes around glaciers in the upper alpine zone of eastern Nepal. Like *Saxifraga pulvinaria,* it forms a cushion, but usually thinner and freer because of severe winds. The cushion is 3–7 cm thick, larger and thicker on stable stony slopes but only 1 cm thick on the unstable sandy slope seen here, where plants formed discontinuous cushions, or mats. The leaves resemble those of *Sagina,* or pearlwort, but are much smaller and harder, 3–5 mm long, less than 1 mm wide, with blunt tip. The flowers are 5–7 mm across, usually stalkless, sometimes with hairy stalks to 5 mm long. 26 July 1990, S of Mt. Makalu, alt. 4950 m, E Nepal

Bergenia purpurascens (Hook. f. & Thoms.) Engl.   Saxifragaceae

Garden bergenias derive mainly from *Bergenia stracheyi,* which grows in dry regions of western Himalaya and adjacent Central Asia. *Bergenia purpurascens* grows in wet regions of eastern Himalaya and south-western China. From a thick underground rootstock, the plant reaches 15–30 cm tall. The ovate leaves are 8–15 cm long and roughly toothed on their margins. The magenta flowers are 1.5–2 cm long. The plants seen here grow on a mossy slope under *Rhododendron fulgens,* forming a herbaceous community with yellow-flowered *Caltha palustris* var. *himalensis* and white-flowered *Primula obliqua.* 21 July 1990, SE of Mt. Makalu, alt. 4100 m, E Nepal

Potentilla fruticosa var. _pumila_ Hook. f.   Rosaceae

The shrubby cinquefoil seen here growing on the tops of gravel hills left behind by retreating glaciers has been dwarfed to 5 cm tall and, because the wind is so strong, the compound leaves are not open completely. Long-haired, lanceolate, and hard-surfaced, the leaves usually have five leaflets, each 6–10 mm long and linear-oblong. Narrow leaf petioles have brown papery stipules that envelop the small branches. The bright yellow flowers are 2.5–3 cm in diameter. The inner surface of the calyx is the same color as the rounded petals. 3 August 1989, E of Chukung, Khumbu, alt. 5200 m, E Nepal

Potentilla coriandrifolia D. Don   Rosaceae

This is an annoying plant to photograph because of its spreading habit and the tendency of the white flowers to glow in the strong sunshine. It grows in dry pastures and has a thick, very deep rootstock. One to three flowers bloom at the tips of stems 8–15 cm long. Leaves with their stalks are 5–10 cm long and are much dissected like the leaf of coriander, hence the name. The flowers are 1.5–2 cm across with a dark red center. Glossy elliptic leaves in the lower right of the photo are a dwarf *Salix* species. The snow-covered mountain in the background is Mt. Makalu (8463 m). 5 August 1990, SE of Mt. Makalu, alt. 4450 m, E Nepal

Potentilla tapetodes Soják   Rosaceae

This rather rare cinquefoil grows on wind-blown stony hills of the upper alpine zone in northern Bhutan and southeastern Tibet. It is often included in *Potentilla microphylla,* but it differs in having much smaller leaves with fewer lobes and almost stalkless flowers. It always forms a tight cushion. A hard woody rootstock delves underground, sometimes forming a large cushion over rocks. The pinnate leaves are 7–15 mm long, including short stalks, and 6–8 mm wide. The flowers measure 1.2–1.5 cm across. The cushion of the plant in the photo is rooting atop a mound already made up by a grass of the sedge family. 30 June 1992, SE of Lunana, alt. 5200 m, N Bhutan

Spongiocarpella purpurea (Li) Yakovlev   Leguminosae

The variable flowers of this species are red at higher elevations (upper photo) and yellow elsewhere (lower photo), and the two colors never appear together. The thin but tough rootstock breaks out from the gravelly soil forming an island-shaped mat 10–30 cm in diameter. The pinnate compound leaves are covered with hairs. During flowering, they are 2–4 cm long, but afterwards they lengthen. The flowers are 2–2.5 cm long, including the densely haired, cylindrical calyx. This plant is also known by the name *Chesneya nubigena*. (Upper) 29 June 1992, SE of Lunana, alt. 5250 m, N Bhutan; (Lower) 9 July 1991, E of Num La, Dolpo, alt. 4800 m, W Nepal

Thermopsis barbata Royle   Leguminosae

These curious-looking perennials are densely covered with long hairs and clusters of chocolate-brown flowers. They are found growing on stony grasslands and in overgrazed pastures near temporary settlements for livestock. The plant has a stout rootstock underground, forming a large rounded clump 30–50 cm tall. Flowers begin to open at an early stage of annual growth, with leaves opening after flowering has finished. The flowers are 2.5–3 cm long, with erect stalks. The snowy mountain in the background of the photo is Mt. Jichu Drake (6809 m). 11 June 1992, near Lingshi Dzong, alt. 4100 m, N Bhutan

Geranium pratense L. Geraniaceae

This geranium, known by the common name meadow cranesbill, is distributed widely across temperate Eurasia from Europe to China, and colonizes pastures and irrigation banks in the dry western Himalayas. The 20- to 40-cm tall plant has long-stalked leaves, which have five to seven diamond-shaped lobes and are 3–5.5 cm across. Flowers open one after the other in pairs at the tips of the flexible stems. The flowers are 2.5–4 cm in diameter. Glandular hairs on the flower stems and calyces are somewhat sticky to the touch. The plant in the photo is sheltered and warmed by rocks, and has grown unusually large. 1 August 1993, SW of Mt. Nanga Parbat, alt. 4200 m, N Pakistan

Stellera chamaejasme L.   Thymelaeaceae

Grazing goats, sheep, and yaks ignore this species, so these plants have become quite large and look as if they had been cultivated by nearby villagers. This unusual herbaceous perennial grows in arid, rocky valleys and sparse coniferous woods. Its numerous stems branch out from a thick rootstock. The plant reaches 15–20 cm tall, and its alternate leaves are 1.5–2 cm long. The stalkless flowers are 7–15 mm long and 5–7 mm wide, usually white inside and maroon outside. A variety with yellow-orange flowers is prevalent in southwestern China. The stupas in the background belong to the Bon, an old religious group. 28 June 1991, near Ringmo, Phoksumdo, alt. 3550 m, W Nepal

Cortia depressa (D. Don) Norman   Umbelliferae

This stemless plant protects itself from strong winds and cold nights by pressing its compound umbels of white flowers to the flat gravelly soil. The whole plant measures 15 cm across. A ring of white umbels surrounds the central large umbel of dark red juvenile fruits. The stalks of these umbels are reddish. The leaf stalks are hidden beneath the inflo-rescences, and only the tips of the pinnate leaves are visible. Yellow-green plants in the photo are *Arenaria ciliolata;* dark-green linear-lanceolate leaves in the upper left are a *Saxifraga* species; leaf rosettes in the lower left are a *Gentiana* species. 21 September 1993, near Tampe La, upstream of Nikachu, alt. 4400 m, C Bhutan

Cassiope fastigiata (Wall.) D. Don   Ericaceae

Under a subalpine forest of rhododendrons, junipers, birches, and rowans, this evergreen shrublet has become a large clump. It is common in mossy areas with high summer rainfall from subalpine to lower alpine regions. The plant is 15–30 cm tall and its woody stems divide and grow as they touch the ground. The tiny leaves are densely packed in four rows on stems that rise at their tips. The thick, ovate leaves are 4–5 mm long. The flower stalks emerge from between the leaves and carry hanging single bell-shaped flowers, which are 7 mm long. The lower, older leaves have turned black and persist on the stems. 15 June 1989, NE of Junbesi, Solu, alt. 3800 m, E Nepal

Rhododendron aeruginosum Hook. f. Ericaceae

Smaller but similar to shrubby relatives _Rhododendron campanulatum_ and _R. wallichii,_ this species grows profusely on north-faced slopes of the lower alpine zone in northern Bhutan. It measures 0.5–2 m tall. The elliptic leaves are 6–8 cm long, somewhat matted above, and densely covered with reddish-brown velvety hairs beneath, with recurved margins. Campanulate flowers on reddish stalks have magenta-red corollas 2.5–3 cm long. Local residents call the plant "kehm" and use the leaves to roll cigarettes after rubbing off the velvety hairs. A ridge of Table Mountain can be seen in the upper part of the photo. 27 June 1992, E of Thanza, Lunana, alt. 4400 m, N Bhutan

Rhododendron nivale Hook. f.   Ericaceae

No other rhododendron grows at a higher elevation. While almost all rhododendrons prefer acid soil, this dwarf species grows profusely on hills covered with limestone crags exposed to dry wind and full sunshine, up to 5500 m. It varies from 5 to 50 cm in height. The leaves are ovate and, at 4–8 mm long, probably the smallest in this genus. Their upper surfaces are dark green and densely covered in scales that gleam silvery in the light. The five-lobed flowers open flatly with a diameter of 1.5–1.8 cm. There are 10 stamens, which are hairy at their bases. The long red style is erect. 29 June 1992, lakeside of Tsorim, E of Lunana, alt. 5250 m, N Bhutan

Rhododendron arboreum Smith   Ericaceae

The well-known Himalayan scenic spot Poon Hill is a haze of red in late April when rhododendrons are entirely covered in bloom. This grove of _Rhododendron_ likely began when humans cut down all the dominant firs; livestock left the rhododendrons uneaten because the young leaves are poisonous when shoots are growing. This is undoubtedly the most common rhododendron species seen in the Himalayas. It is also the tallest, reaching 20 m tall, with trunks up to 1 m in diameter in the damp native groves of giant firs. Because it is so adaptable and capable of being cultivated at lower altitudes, it has been used to develop many garden hybrids since it was introduced to Europe in the 19th cen-

tury. *Rhododendron arboreum* is the national flower of Nepal where it is called "Lali Gurans." The leaves are 8–17 cm long, tough, and leathery with deeply etched lateral veining. Their undersides are usually covered in light brown feltlike hairs. The flower is 4–5 cm long and pink to crimson, rarely white. The gray brown bark exfoliates in vertical oblong flakes. In the background, the large mountain on the left is Dhaulagiri (8167 m). The pointed mountain on the right is Tukuche Peak (6920 m). 3 May 1989, W of Ghorapani, alt. 3000 m, C Nepal

Androsace tapete Maxim. Primulaceae

It takes at least ten years from first budding for this plant to form a rounded cushion about 8 cm high and 25 cm wide in the limestone gravel at arid heights. Both the individual flowers and the rosettes are 3–4 mm in diameter. Underneath the new rosette is a pillar of numerous older rosettes linked together with a thin perennial stem. Each pillar is repeatedly divided into branches, which are so crowded together that, even when pressed firmly by hand, the surface of the plant does not give. The leaves are 2 mm long. The inside leaves of the rosette appear white because they are covered in long hairs. 10 July 1991, SE of Shey Gompa, Dolpo, alt. 4700 m, W Nepal

Androsace selago Klatt   Primulaceae

Compared with its near relative *Androsace tapete,* this species grows on wetter stony slopes of the upper alpine zone from Sikkim to Bhutan. The plant in the photo has formed a somewhat open cushion 13 cm in diameter and 7 cm tall. Due to the softness of the dense hairs around the edges and undersides of the leaves, you can depress the surface slightly with a finger. The rosettes of leaves measure 3–5 mm in diameter. Individual leaves are 2.5–3 mm long. The large, short-stalked flowers are 5–8 mm in diameter and cover the rosettes when they bloom. The center of the white flowers is yellow green. 29 June 1992, lakeside of Tsorim, E of Lunana, alt. 5200 m, N Bhutan

Androsace globifera Duby   Primulaceae

This plant grew as if it were trying to cover over the depressions of the
mossy banks. The cushion is as supple as a wet sponge and feels almost warm to the touch. In spite of the species name, the rosette is
not as globose as that of *Androsace robusta*. The densely clustered,
upright leaves are 3–5 mm long and 1 mm wide. Their tips are covered
in fine hairs. The flowers are 5–7 mm in diameter on short, thin stems.
They are pink with paler margins and yellow-green centers. A bloom of
Gypsophylla cerastioides, a member of the carnation family, has
strayed into the upper right corner of the photo. 4 July 1992, S of Tampe
La, upstream of Nikachu, alt. 4500 m, C Bhutan

Androsace robusta (Knuth) Hand.-Mazz.   Primulaceae

Long known as *Androsace muscoides* forma *longiscapa* but since 1997 identified as a possible subspecies of *Androsace robusta,* this cushion former grows on dry, stony slopes. The oblong to lanceolate leaves are 3–8 mm long, with dense long hairs around the tip of under surfaces. Flowering stems are erect to 5 cm tall with three to seven flowers, which are 6–8 mm across. The plant in the photo grows on bare screes of the upper alpine zone where it has formed a mat of tightly closed rosettes connected to each other with short runners. It is smaller than typical and was covered with snow the previous night. 21 June 1988, W of Thorung Pass, Annapurna Himal, alt. 4650 m, C Nepal

Primula megalocarpa Hara   Primulaceae

This primrose grows on stony slopes of valley heads in eastern Himalaya, often profuse beside streams that appear after continuous rains. At 5–10 cm tall, they are short, but overall they are thick with well-developed root systems extending deep into the ground. The inner leaves, which emerge after the late snows melt, are oblong to oblanceolate, 4–7 cm long, and finely toothed. Their edges tend to recurve. The flowers are 2–2.5 cm wide with each rounded corolla lobe overlapping. The flowers are pink or white, but it is unusual for plants of different colors to grow near one another as they do in this photo. 1 July 1990, N of Topke Gola, alt. 4400 m, E Nepal

Primula sikkimensis Hook. f.   Primulaceae

The most common primrose in the eastern Himalayas has a robust fig-
ure, 20–70 cm tall, and bell-shaped pendulous yellow flowers, both of
which differ greatly from the potted primroses known in cultivation. In
the wild, plants form big clumps besides streams, but sometimes colonize entire pastures with smaller clumps. The leaves are 5–15 cm
long and have finely toothed margins. The flowers are 1.3–2 cm in diameter and slightly fragrant, with white farina inside the corolla. The
mix of flowers in the photo includes yellow *Ranunculus brotherusii,*
pink *Geranium donianum,* and a white *Juncus* species. 17 July 1988,
SE of Ghunsa, Mt. Kangchenjunga, alt. 4100 m, E Nepal

Primula wollastonii Balf. f.   Primulaceae

A. F. R. Wollaston collected this species in Tibet during the first Mt. Everest expedition in 1921. Since then, it has been found in several places in Nepal near the world's highest mountain. It grows abundantly on thick pastures of wind-blown hilly slopes of Khumbu, where it has longer scapes and wider flowers than plants growing on cliff banks.

The plant measures 10–20 cm tall. The leaves are obovate to oblanceolate, 2–4 cm long, covered with long and somewhat stiff hairs above. The two to five flowers are stalkless, drooping, and 1.5–2 cm across. The leaf undersides and flower clusters are covered in farina. 30 July 1990, SE of Mt. Makalu, alt. 4500 m, E Nepal

Primula stuartii Wall.   Primulaceae

After the late snow melts, this plant suddenly emerges from the accumulation of old foliage, raising up thick scapes with rounded inflorescences. The scapes are 15–30 cm tall. The flower buds open one after
another beginning with the outer row. The sweetly scented flowers
open face out and have five lobes. The thick base of each lobe is rich
yellow; the thinner tip is paler and notable for its finely fringed edges.
The narrow oblanceolate leaves are 10–20 cm long with dark green upper surface and finely serrated edges. The leaf undersides and flower
clusters are covered in yellow farina. 23 June 1990, near Sabha
Pokhari, Jaljale Himal, alt. 4300 m, E Nepal

Primula strumosa Balf. f. & Cooper
Primula obliqua W. W. Smith   Primulaceae

As a herd of yaks passed by, I realized that this pasture of yellow-flow-ered *Primula strumosa* and white-flowered *Primula obliqua* is not just the product of a unique mountain environment, but also of the cen-turies-old eating habits of yaks, which spurn these primroses. *Primula*

strumosa, sometimes treated as a subspecies of *P. calderiana,* which is very similar except for its purple flowers and drier habitat, grows on the moist southern slopes of eastern Himalaya. The plant measures 15–25 cm tall in flowering, with yellow farina. The leaf blades are elliptic to oblanceolate, 5–15 cm long, with veins impressed above, and with

toothed margins likely to recurve. The corolla is open to saucer shape, 1.5–2.5 cm across, yellow with an orange center. *Primula obliqua,* with a similar distribution pattern, measures 20–35 cm tall and has yellow farina and thick bud scales at the base. The leaf blades are oblong to oblanceolate, 15–20 cm long with toothed margins. The flowers are pendant and sometimes fragrant. The corolla is thick, opening to a parasol-like shape, 2–3 cm across, usually white, often tinged with carmine-red. Two dwarf *Rhododendron* species with red and white flowers can be seen among the ponds. 25 June 1990, S of Gosa, Jaljale Himal, alt. 4150 m, E Nepal

Primula concinna Watt   Primulaceae

This extremely small primrose is 5–15 mm tall with flowers only 5–8 mm in diameter. Growing in thin soils of gravelly terrain that is often swept by cold, drizzling rain, it forms small mats spreading out from entangled fine roots in the mold of mosses and ground covers. One to three flowers appear on each stem. The obovate or oblanceolate leaves are 0.5–2 cm long with stalks, and have roughly toothed margins. Yellow farina covers their undersides and the calyces. The white stringlike ground-covering lichen in the photo is a *Thamnolia* species. A sedum relative, *Rhodiola bupleuroides,* is in flower in the upper left. 12 July 1989, near Gokyo, Khumbu, alt. 4800 m, E Nepal

Primula tenuiloba (Watt) Pax   Primulaceae

This small primrose also forms small mats on mosses and other ground covers in moist gravelly areas. The leaves have broad stalks. They are ovate, 2.5–5 mm long, and have fine teeth on their margins much like the teeth on a comb. The slender flower stems rise 5–10 mm from the midst of the leaves. There is one 12- to 18-mm-wide flower at the tip of each stem. The flowers are pale purple to pale pink with a white center. The flower tubes are 7–12 mm long, and they are covered in soft white hairs inside and out. The green calyces are one-third the length of the flower tubes. There is no farina. 7 July 1990, NW of Topke Gola, alt. 4600 m, E Nepal

Primula capitata Hook.   Primulaceae

This curious primrose grows in damp pastures and among low shrubs where it reaches 13–25 cm tall. Disk-shaped inflorescences, 2.5–3 cm in diameter, form at the tip of the thick flower stems. In the photo, which was taken from above, only the outer rows of flowers in each inflorescence are opened. The upper flowers remain sheathed in their calyces and most dry up without opening. The opened flowers are pendent and 1 cm in diameter. The toothed leaves are 3–5 cm long and finely veined. They are entirely covered in farina that is heaviest on their undersides and on the tip of the flower stems. 18 July 1988, beside Yalung Glacier, SW of Mt. Kangchenjunga, alt. 4500 m, E Nepal

Primula deuteronana Craib   Primulaceae

Colonizing in deep leaf mold on slopes where the snowmelt is late, this primrose has deep veining in the 2.5- to 4-cm-long leaves, which are sharply and irregularly toothed on their margins and covered with farina on their undersides. Many old blackened leaves remain at the plant base. Instead of developed flower stems, pedicels 1–2 cm long come directly from the base. Each plant bears one to three flowers that are 2.5 cm in diameter at most and have a white tube 1.5–2 cm long. The corolla lobe is elliptical with irregular notches on its tip. Among the primroses are the silky-haired young leaves of a *Potentilla* species.
21 June 1990, at Dossan, Jaljale Himal, alt. 4100 m, E Nepal

Gentiana waltonii Burk.   Gentianaceae

(Upper photograph) Blooming on dry, rocky crags behind a famous monastery, this gentian is 15–20 cm tall with clumping, narrow leaves 8–12 cm long. The flowers are 3.5 cm long and 2 cm in diameter with purple-brown calyces. Five green calyx lobes open outward. 19 August 1992, near Drepung, W of Lhasa, alt. 4300 m, C Tibet

Gentiana emodi Marq. ex Sealy   Gentianaceae

(Lower photograph) Looking like purple jewels in the gravel, these flowers are 1.5–1.8 cm wide and 2 cm long. The tough leathery leaves are 2–5 mm long, folded inwards on the central vein, forming tight, symmetrical, elaborate lozenge-shaped rosettes. 15 August 1988, NW of Yangma, Kangchenjunga Himal, alt. 4650 m, E Nepal

Gentiana ornata (G. Don) Griseb.   Gentianaceae

After the long monsoon period has ended and the majority of plants have finished flowering, the glaciated distant peaks become visible in the clear blue sky, and the advent of drying winds brings colonies of this autumn gentian into bloom. The 5- to 10-cm-long flower stems rest on the ground with many narrow leaves; each stem bears a single flower 3–3.5 cm in diameter. The pale blue corolla has deep purple and yellowish stripes on the outside. The white pyramidal peak of Mt. Langtang Lirung (7245 m) can be seen in the upper part of the photo with a minor peak of Ghenge Liru (6581 m) at the left. 3 October 1988, near Laurebina, W of Gosainkund, alt. 3950 m, C Nepal

Swertia wardii Marq.   Gentianaceae

This magnificent perennial, a relative of marsh felwort (*Swertia peren-nis*), grows luxuriantly on steep, wet lake banks where it competes with *Potentilla, Cirsium,* and shrubby rhododendrons. The thick, upright stems are 30–70 cm tall. The 3-cm-wide pale purple flowers, which are large for the genus, make it a standout. At the base of each of the five corolla lobes are sets of dark purple long-haired dots which are the sites of the plant's nectar. The oblanceolate basal leaves have stalks and are 12–15 cm long. During the week I spent in this mountainous region, I never once saw the sun. 21 September 1993, S of Tampe La, up-stream of Nikachu, alt. 4300 m, C Bhutan

Acantholimon lycopodioides (Girard) Boiss.   Plumbaginaceae

Reminiscent of a hedgehog with its upright bristles, this shrublet forms dense, rounded cushions 20–50 cm across on dry, stony slopes of Central Asia. The old brown leaves persist on tough woody stems inside the plant. The 1.5- to 2-cm-long needlelike foliage clusters at the ends of the stems and is pointed at the tip. The flowers are 5 mm in diameter with white calyces. Their upper sections are shaped like closed umbrellas with five dark brown streaks resembling the umbrella frame. When the plant is ready to disperse its seeds, these umbrellas open wide. 18 July 1993, N of Deosai Plains, alt. 3800, N Pakistan

Chionocharis hookeri (C. B. Clarke) I. M. Johnston   Boraginaceae

This plant is a cushion in every sense of the word; not only is it pillow shaped, but it feels soft and spongy to the touch. It forms 5- to 20-cm-wide soft cushions from place to place on the upper alpine gravel. Height is usually 3–5 cm. Small leaves are covered with woolly hairs on their upper surfaces and gathered into rosettes 7–10 mm wide. The leaves are upright and tightly pressed together, never opening fully out. The flowers are 6–8 mm across. The hairy, pinnate leaves of the cinquefoil relative *Potentilla tapetodes,* which is rooted into the plant seen here, appear in the upper right corner of the photo. 29 June 1992, near Tsorim, SE of Lunana, alt. 5200 m, N Bhutan

Onosma hookeri C. B. Clarke   Boraginaceae

This perennial grows on unstable grassy slopes or cliffs of arid areas where the long roots stretch deeply underground. The entire 10- to 25-cm-tall plant is covered in bristles that are rough to the touch. The flower buds, which are tightly gathered in a scorpion shape, open one by one. The flowers are so heavy they weigh the stems down. The lin-ear leaves are 2–10 cm. The tubular corolla is 2–2.5 cm long and mauve colored, variously tinged with red. Its outer sides are covered in soft hairs. The reddish purple juice extracted from rootstocks of this species is locally used by monks for dyeing paper and butter offerings. 25 June 1992, in Lunana, alt. 3700 m, N Bhutan

Phlomis rotata Benth. ex Hook. f.   Labiatae

This phlomis grows on sand, as shown here, and on exposed grassy slopes of the upper alpine zone. The thick leaves are 5–12 cm long and wide as they spread out in crosslike opposition on very short stems. This habit prevents wind damage, keeps competing plants away, and allows the leaves to absorb sufficient sunlight in daytime for photo- synthesis and enough warmth from the ground to prevent sudden freezing at night. The inflorescence is less than 10 cm tall and has spines on the bracts and calyces that are painful to the touch. The corolla is 1.2–1.5 cm long with soft hairs on the inside of the upper lip. 29 July 1989, near Gorakshep, Khumbu, alt. 5200 m, E Nepal

Eriophyton wallichii Benth.   Labiatae

This peculiar, 10- to 15-cm-tall plant protects its flowers from drizzle and sleet with a woolly cape. The lower half of the thick square stems is sunk between rocks. The broadly ovate, closely layered, opposite leaves are 3–4 cm long, veined, and covered with dense, long hairs. The leaf tips are roughly toothed. The 2- to 2.5-cm-long flowers lack peti- oles. The corollas emerge from upright calyces and bend to face out- ward. The large upper lip is rounded and hooded. It is yellow-brown to red-purple, and its upper surface is covered in soft hairs. Pale yellow flowers around the plant are *Anaphalis cavei*. 26 August 1991, near Yala, Langtang Himal, alt. 4500 m, C Nepal

Lagotis species

Scrophulariaceae

Despite some differences, this plant seems to have a close affinity with the polymorphic species *Lagotis kunawurensis* and it might be included in this species. This low-growing plant is prevalent in the flat glacial moraine in the northern Khumbu area. The flower stems range from 4 to 10 cm tall, but they spread out along the ground and only the 2- to 5- cm-long inflorescences rise upright. The leaves are 3–6 cm long and ovate. Their lateral veining is slightly impressed, and they are coarsely toothed on their margins. The flowers are 1–1.2 cm long with small bracts at their bases. 20 July 1989, S of Nangpa La, Khumbu, alt. 5200 m, E Nepal

Lagotis kunawurensis (Royle ex Benth.) Rupr.   Scrophulariaceae

This variable species is widely found throughout the Himalayas in damp gravelly soil of valley heads. The flowers, leaves, and bracts vary in shape from place to place. The plant in the photo seems to be a typical form; it is 20 cm tall and has an inflorescence 6–8 cm long. The leaf stalk is 5–7 cm long and is buried in the earth. The flowers are 8–10 mm long. In the area where the photo was taken, all the flowers were white, but, in other areas, light blue and light purple ones are common. White hairy leaves of *Saussurea falconeri* and *Artemisia* species can be seen in the lower left of the photo. 16 July 1993, western rim of Deosai Plains, alt. 4000 m, N Pakistan

Veronica lanuginosa Benth. ex Hook. f. Scrophulariaceae

The 6- to 8-mm tiny cobalt blue flowers peek out from inflorescences that are so covered in woolly hairs they appear to be covered lightly with snow. The numerous short (3–5 cm) flower stems stand upright on a craggy slope overlooking a glacier. The plant sends out runners which form small colonies in the gravelly soil. The stalkless, opposite leaves are obovate in shape and are 5–10 mm long. Plants growing among rocks are larger. The corolla is deeply four-lobed and the lobes are overlapping. A dwarf form of _Rhodiola bupleuroides_ can be seen in the center left corner of the photo. 2 July 1992, S of Rinchenzoe, upstream of Mangde Chu, alt. 5200 m, N Bhutan

Pedicularis bicornuta Klotzsch   Scrophulariaceae

Even hungry goats won't eat this lousewort whose thick, upright, 15- to 40-cm stems rise impressively out of colonies on dry pasture slopes and in the midst of grass banks along irrigation ditches. The plant also grows on stable rocky slopes of high mountains as shown in the photo. The pinnate lower leaves are 8–15 cm long and 2 cm wide. More than 30 yellow flowers bloom per stem, opening from the top down all summer long. The white tubular portion of the corolla emerges beyond the inflated calyx. Two of the three lobes of the lower lips are rounded and 1 cm long, curling up to conceal a small upper lip. 15 July 1993, northern rim of Deosai Plains, alt. 4150 m, N Pakistan

Pedicularis longiflora* var. *tubiformis (Klotzsch) Tsoong   Scrophulariaceae

This lousewort has orange-yellow, narrow flower tubes that rise like the necks of giraffes. It is found along the spine of the Himalayas into northern Tibet and colonizes in moist soils such as those around seeps. The lower part of the 7- to 15-cm stem is prostrate. The basal leaves have long stalks. The pinnately lobed leaves are 2–5 cm long. The upper lip of the corolla narrows to the twisted beak like a pig's tail. The lower lip is 1.5 cm wide with three lobes that are shallowly notched at the tip. Two red dots are visible on the base of the central lobe. Mt. Merra (6344 m) can be seen in the upper center of the photo. 5 August 1988, near Kambachen, Kangchenjunga Himal, alt. 4000 m, E Nepal

Pedicularis cheilanthifolia Schrenk   Scrophulariaceae

Most louseworts prefer dense grasslands because of their parasitic nature, but this species, common on alpine slopes of the western Himalaya and Karakoram, can survive even on bare screes, forming a small colony. The plant measures 7–20 cm tall, with several stems that are covered with long white hairs. The basal leaves have slender stalks, and the stem leaves are whorled. The flowers are 2.3–2.5 cm long, in terminal dense clusters. The white to pink corolla has a tube as long as or slightly longer than the calyx. The rocky peaks that form the southern rim of Karakoram can be seen in the background of the photo. 6 July 1993, W of Thalle La, Baltistan, alt. 4400 m, N Pakistan

Pedicularis cornigera Yamazaki   Scrophulariaceae

(Upper photograph) This lousewort is 5–15 cm tall with short, branched stems and 2- to 4-cm-long densely alternate leaves. It has a 4- to 5-cm narrow corolla tube. The large lower lip is shallowly three-lobed, rounded, and inclined to one side. It conceals the curved upper lip. 15 August 1988, NW of Yangma, Kangchenjunga Himal, alt. 4650 m, E Nepal

Pedicularis nepalensis Prain   Scrophulariaceae

(Lower photograph) This lousewort is 4–8 cm tall and appears as solitary plants in open slopes and in the shadows of rocky outcrops. The magenta-red flowers have an enlarged lower lip that is semi-circular, three-lobed, and 1.8–2 cm wide. It does not conceal the upper lip. 8 August 1988, N of Nango La, Kangchenjunga Himal, alt. 4550 m, E Nepal

Oreosolen wattii Hook. f.   Scrophulariaceae

The soft 2- to 5-cm-long stems of this dwarf perennial burrow straight down into the mold of mosses growing between the rocks. The hairless leaves are opposite and spread flatly on the ground in the shape of a cross which allows them to avoid cold winds. The 1.7- to 2-cm-long bright yellow flowers stand erect to attract pollinators. The 2- to 4-cm-long leaves have coarsely toothed margins and deeply impressed veining. The corolla tube is two-lipped, the upper being larger and two lobed, the lower shorter and three lobed. These lobes bend inwardly and close like a clenched fist when misty rains begin. 20 July 1989, S of Nangpa La, Khumbu, alt. 5200 m, E Nepal

Hippolytia gossypina (Hook. f. & Thoms. ex C. B. Clarke) Shih Compositae

Growing profusely on slopes of damp glacial moraine, this species spreads in all directions. It is easy to spot the clusters of silvery foliage, but it is rather rare to find a flowering plant. The plant forms mats or cushions, with a well-branched woody rootstock and many blackened old leaves. The whole plant is covered with white woolly hairs looking like fresh snow. The flowering stems are 2–4 cm tall, with several flower heads crowded flatly at the top. The flower heads are 5–8 mm across and consist of minute orange-yellow tubular flowers opening from outer ones. *Tanacetum gossypinum* is a synonym for this species. 2 September 1991, S of Ganja La, Langtang Himal, alt. 4350 m, C Nepal

Allardia glabra Decne.   Compositae

The reason these flowers growing in this barren, glacial moraine are so showy—they look as if they had escaped from a garden—is perhaps to lure pollinators to a place so dangerous they might freeze and be unable to escape. The tips of the rosette leaves are palmate and three to seven lobed. Their length is 7–12 mm. Flowers are solitary on short stems 2–4 cm across with pink or white ray florets and a large yellow disk. The Sherpas of the Khumbu area gather and dry the leaves, which they mix with juniper leaves to burn as an insect repellent. *Waldheimia glabra* is a frequently encountered synonym. 26 July 1990, beside Barun Glacier, S of Mt. Makalu, alt. 5100 m, E Nepal

Cremanthodium ellisii (Hook. f.) Kitam. Compositae

This species in its broadest sense varies in plant size, number of flower heads, leaf shape, and hairiness, with a wide range of distribution in dry areas of Himalaya, including Tibet and western China. It often grows on screes or bare grounds with deep clayish soil underground containing enough water even during the dry weather. The plant in the photo was growing on a dry, wind-blown scree and was extremely dwarfed with thick, dark-colored, and hairy leaves; it reached 7 cm in height and had solitary flowers 4–4.5 cm across. In milder habitats, the stems are 15–40 cm tall with a few flower heads. 16 August 1992, near Karo La, E of Gyantse, alt. 5200 m, S Tibet

Achillea millefolium L. Compositae

These tall perennials with white flowers are known as yarrow. Here, they grow along stone walls of a field in the westernmost Himalaya with bladder campions, red clovers, alfalfas, and sickle-medicks as if they were planted in a border garden. All are widespread over dry temperate Eurasia. The species measures 30–50 cm tall. Terminal flower clusters are 5–12 cm across, with many flower heads, which are 6–7 mm across and consist of usually five ray florets. The main peak of Nanga Parbat (8126 m), in the left background, looks much lower than Rakhiot Peak (7074 m) to the right; clouds covered both. 29 July 1993, near Tarshing, E of Mt. Nanga Parbat, alt. 2950 m, N Pakistan

Richteria pyrethroides Kar. & Kir. Compositae

While waiting for these flowers to stop swaying in the wind, I was aware of bits of soil and rock that were crumbling beneath my feet and falling down the steep slope to the glacier below. Numerous stems 15–20 cm long branch out from the woody rootstock. The 2- to 5-cm-long leaves are alternate near the base of the stems. Each stem has one terminal flower, which is 3–4 cm in diameter. As the flower fades, the white ray petals droop and the stem continues to grow. This species has the well-known synonym *Chrysanthemum pyrethroides*. In the background of the photo is a pyramidal ridge of Toshain Peak (6325 m). 31 July 1993, near Shaigiri, S of Mt. Nanga Parbat, alt. 4050 m, N Pakistan

Soroseris hookeriana (C. B. Clarke) Stebbins   Compositae

This unique perennial has compact flower clusters at the top of thick, hollow stems. The stem is widened at the top, just below the flower clusters, presumably to keep respiration heat produced by the plant itself as well as warmth absorbed from daytime sunshine. The plant measures 3–10 cm tall and is covered with woolly hairs around flower clusters that measure 4–5 cm across. The 40–60 flower heads are 3–4 mm across, with four yellow ray florets, which have five teeth at the truncate apex. The western face of Pemthan Ri (6758 m) can be seen in the upper part of the photo. 24 August 1991, right bank of Langtang Glacier, alt. 4600 m, C Nepal

Aster diplostephioides (DC.) C. B. Clarke   Compositae

As I waited to take this photo, thick clouds cleared for a few minutes, revealing the world's third highest mountain—Mt. Kangchenjunga (8586 m)—against a blue sky. This aster is 5–20 cm tall with solitary flower heads 5–8 cm across. The woody rootstock and roots are well developed. The lanceolate leaves are 2–5 cm long and mostly entire. The pink ray florets have very narrow, 1- to 2-mm-wide petals which reflex as the flowers age and are likely to vibrate with a breeze as seen in the photo. Sticky glandular hairs cover the upper stem and the involucral bracts. 30 July 1988, Pangpema, N of Mt. Kangchenjunga, alt. 5100 m, E Nepal

Anaphalis xylorhiza Sch. Bip. ex Hook. f.   Compositae

No other *Anaphalis* species grows at a higher altitude. This species is at home on old moraines covered with thick accumulation of withered plants, exposed to strong and dry winds. The twisted woody rootstock is like a thick wire rope spreading shallowly underground. It forms a dense and extensive tuft of erect yellowish-green leaves covered with woolly hairs. The plant measures 3–8 cm tall, with compact terminal flower clusters 1.5–2 cm across. These clusters consist of 5–10 flower heads, each 6–7 mm across when fully open under the direct sunshine. 24 July 1990, near Shershon, S of Mt. Makalu, alt. 4550 m, E Nepal

Anaphalis nepalensis (Spreng.) Hand.-Mazz.   Compositae

In cold rain, the just-opened white flower heads tend to close up in the shape of candle flames. Abundant in dry regions of western Himalaya, this variable species, also known as *Anaphalis triplinervis* var. *intermedia,* is difficult to distinguish from closely related species. The new stems in the photo are 12–15 cm long. The fallen stems will form new rootstocks. Narrow leaves are 2–2.5 cm long and covered with woolly hairs on both sides. The flower heads are 1.5 cm wide when the white involucral bracts fully open. At higher elevations, the stems are shorter and bear only one flower head each. 10 August 1993, near Fairy Meadow, N of Mt. Nanga Parbat, alt. 3800 m, N Pakistan

Leontopodium monocephalum Edgew. Compositae

Due to the fog that had rolled in before dawn, this edelweiss sparkled like a jewel when it was finally lit by the sun. It forms a mat with a narrow, branched, widely spreading rootstock that produces either rosette leaves or flowering stems. The plant is 2–7 cm tall. The densely woolly involucral leaves and the basal rosette leaves are only 5–15 mm long.

The flower heads are 5–6 mm in diameter. This photo displays a small plant with solitary flower heads. Larger plants may have several smaller flower heads. The whole plant tends to golden yellow when it dries up. No other *Leontopodium* grows at a higher altitude. 26 July 1990, right bank of Barun Glacier, S of Mt. Makalu, alt. 4950 m, E Nepal

Leontopodium jacotianum Beauverd   Compositae

The most common Himalayan edelweiss grows on alpine stony slopes, forming a tuft of leaves and flowering stems with well-branched slender rootstock, on which many withered leaves remain. The narrow, 1-cm-long involucral leaves radiate from the tip of the flowering stems like twinkling stars and are covered with thick woolly hairs on their up-per sides. The rosette leaves and the alternate leaves up the stem are 1–2 cm long. The 4- to 10-cm-tall flowering stems bear several brown-colored flower heads atop the radiating involucral leaves; the central one is larger and is 3–4 mm across. 5 September 1991, right bank of Lirung Glacier, Langtang Himal, alt. 4300 m, C Nepal

Anaphalis cavei Chattarjee   Compositae

This unique species forms a lax, domed cushion covered with woolly hairs like a cobweb. It grows on unstable stony slopes of dry inner valleys. A well-branched slender rootstock, which is about 1 mm across, bears many rosette leaves and several erect flowering stems at the heads. These stems are 3–5 cm tall, tinged with dark purple. The obo-vate to elliptic rosette leaves are 2–5 mm long. Flower clusters measure 1–2 cm across, crowded with 5–10 flower heads, which are 4–7 mm across when fully opened under direct sunshine. Petal-like involucral bracts are creamy yellow and translucent except inner ones. 26 August 1991, near Yala, Langtang Himal, alt. 4500 m, C Nepal

Cirsium falconeri (Hook. f.) Petrak   Compositae

The central flower head in the photo shows the opening of tubular florets in stages. The red florets open from outer ones and incline outwards. Then the pinkish long styles, stained with pollen, emerge from the white tubes of united anthers. The plant is roughly 1 m tall, and the basal leaves are pinnately lobed and 30 cm or more long. The lobes have sharp spines at the tip of each tooth. Many species may yet be split from this variable species in the future. The type specimen collected in Kashmir looks very different from eastern Himalayan plants. 20 September 1993, near Marothang, upstream of Nikachu, alt. 3700 m, C Bhutan

Saussurea gnaphalodes (Royle ex DC.) Sch. Bip.   Compositae

Pale purple flowers appear as the first rays of sunlight melt away the ice covering over the plant. A brownish, warm-looking pappus develops between each tubular flower at bloom time to insulate the reproductive organs from freezing. The 2- to 5-cm-tall plant consists of relatively short flowering stems and rosettes of leaves, both of which emerge from a deep, well-branched rootstock. The oblong leaves reach 1–2.5 cm long and are entirely covered in downy hairs. Terminal flower clusters measure 2–3 cm in diameter and consist of many flower heads about 5 mm in diameter. 2 August 1993, S of Mazeno Pass, W of Mt. Nanga Parbat, alt. 5150 m, N Pakistan

Saussurea gossipiphora D. Don   Compositae

This woolly plant grows on upper alpine screes of eastern Himalaya. As the stems rise, hairs develop from the upright leaves and weave together until a 10- to 20-cm-tall cottonball is formed. Chilly mists dampen the outside of the cottonball, but the room inside remains warm and dry. Large bumblebees can enter this room through a small hole at the top and pollinate flowers even in bad weather. More than 30 flower heads cluster densely on the thick stems; each flower head is 5 mm in diameter. 28 July 1990, southeastern ridge of Mt. Makalu, alt. 5200 m, E Nepal

Saussurea simpsoniana (Field & Gardn.) Lipschitz   Compositae

Domed flower clusters are exposed above reddish-purple woolly hairs on cylindrical flowering stems. This showy plant grows on screes or stony slopes in drier valley heads, forming a tuft of rosette leaves and a few flowering stems from a stout branched rootstock. The flowering stems measure 5–10 cm tall. The linear-oblanceolate basal leaves are 4–6 cm long, and the narrower, shorter upper leaves droop and are thickly covered with woolly hairs. The 20–30 flower heads are 4–6 mm across, with dark purple tubular florets. A mat of white-flowered *Allardia glabra* is in the lower part of the photo. 22 August 1991, W of Pemthang Karpo, Langtang Himal, alt. 4600 m, C Nepal

Saussurea graminifolia Wall. ex DC.   Compositae

In late summer, the upper tips of the purple tubular florets appear to have broken through the dense wool on the top of their tall, hollow flower stems. These florets form a solitary globular flower head 2–2.5 cm across. The flower stems are 10–25 cm tall. Grasslike dark green, narrow leaves rise out of the thick rootstock, forming dense tufts. The leaves are 5–10 cm long and 2 mm wide with impressed midribs. Their margins recurve. The plants pictured here grow with *Primula macro-phylla* and *Rhodiola crenulata* in a shallow depression on a vast scree slope. 29 July 1990, southeastern ridge of Mt. Makalu, alt. 5200 m, E Nepal

Saussurea tridactyla Sch. Bip. ex Hook. f.   Compositae

This species resembles *Saussurea simpsoniana* but is larger and has thicker basal leaves, which are shallowly three to five lobed and broader at the tip. The woolly hairs are never tinted red. Rare in southern slopes of Himalaya but common in northern slopes around Mt. Everest (known in Tibet as Chomolungma), the plant grows on screes or among rocks, from a branched stout rootstock. The aerial part of the cylindrical flowering stem is 6–12 cm tall and 3–5 cm in diameter. Crowded flatly atop the stem are 25–40 flower heads, each 3–4 mm across. Purple tubular florets are slightly exposed from woolly hairs. 1 August 1988, Pangpema, N of Mt. Kangchenjunga, alt. 5000 m, E Nepal

Saussurea bracteata Decne.   Compositae

Large papery bracts cover flower clusters like a greenhouse and serve the same purpose in the severe alpine environment as woolly hairs do on other *Saussurea* species. The plant grows on screes or stony slopes in dry areas of western Himalaya. At flowering, the upper portion of the stem grows enough to expose the flower heads slightly. The plant in the photo is just ready to bloom. The white or pale green, 4- to 5-cm-long boat-shaped bracts sometimes are tinted pink. The plant itself is 20–40 cm tall and entirely covered with soft hairs. The basal leaves measure 6–12 cm long and 1–2 cm wide. 19 July 1993, northern rim of Deosai Plains, alt. 4400 m, N Pakistan

Saussurea obvallata (DC.) Edgew.   Compositae

In northern India these flowers, which resemble lotus flowers when the white bracts are peeled back, are offered up to the gods of the mountains. The bracts never open naturally. Measuring 20–100 cm tall, the plant has lanceolate leaves 20–40 cm long with toothed margins. Flower heads are 1–1.5 cm across in clusters of a few to 15. The species is distributed in disjunct populations and colonizes mostly on rocky slopes. Plants tend to be smaller in drier regions of western Himalaya and taller in wetter regions in the east. In the foreground is *Rhodiola imbricata,* which has just finished flowering. 21 August 1987, below Hemkund, Garhwal, alt. 3900 m, NW India

Allium carolinianum DC.   Alliaceae

Many scattered clumps of this wild onion display their showy pink flowers like garden plants. The species, growing here on a steep, stony
slope of a remote valley, is at home in dry areas of western Himalaya.
A cylindrical bulb, which is buried deeply underground, measures 1.5
cm across and is covered with leathery white sheaths. Flowering stems
are 20–40 cm tall, with several flat and thick leaves near the base. The
flowers are carried in a globular umbel, 2.5–3.5 cm across. The six-part
tubular perianth is closed at its mouth and 5–6 mm long. The style and
stamens protrude slightly from its tips. 18 July 1993, N of Deosai Plains,
alt. 3700 m, N Pakistan

Allium semenovii Regel   Alliaceae

The narrow, cylindrical leaves of this wild onion resemble those of chives and are greatly prized by local herders as a flavorful herb. The plant grows in damp alpine areas of the otherwise dry western Himalayas. Each flowering stem is 15–25 cm tall with a terminal umbel and usually two hollow leaves. The upper leaf rises above the umbels of the orange-yellow flowers, which are 8–15 mm long. The species lacks prominent bulbs, although the basal part of the plant is covered with leaf sheaths buried deeply underground. The deeply five-lobed leaves of *Geranium pratense* can be seen in the background. 15 July 1993, northern rim of Deosai Plains, alt. 4150 m, N Pakistan

Lilium nepalense D. Don   Liliaceae

I first saw this attractive lily after wandering in its habitat for two days following a vague report I had received. I've since found that it is common on wet rocky slopes of temperate oak forests, and I've encountered it many times unexpectedly on the way to alpine areas. The plant measures 40–80 cm long with alternate leaves 5–10 cm long. Flowering stems have a few large flowers at their tips, which cause the stems to lean. The flowers are 8–12 cm wide, pale yellow-green with dark red centers, which glow in prominent bloody red color under the occasional sunshine. 28 June 1989, S of Lukla, Khumbu, alt. 2800 m, E Nepal

Cardiocrinum giganteum (Wall.) Makino   Liliaceae

Scrambling through the mist-soaked undergrowth of ferns, nettles, and balsams in a damp forest of giant evergreen oaks, I came upon this colony of giant lilies. The 1.5- to 2.5-m-tall hollow stems arise from large bulbs deep underground and bear five to ten pure white lilies each. The lower leaves, which are larger than the upper leaves, have long, thick stalks and are a glossy dark green, heart shaped, and 20–25 cm long and wide. The funnel-shaped flowers measure 13–15 cm long with reddish-brown markings. Their intoxicating fragrance fills the air as you approach them. 28 June 1989, S of Lukla, Khumbu, alt. 2800 m, E Nepal

Notholirion macrophyllum (D. Don) Boiss. Liliaceae

Two stems appear to make up the single flower stem in the photo. These reveal the sequential changes of the flowers from top to bottom. First, the tips of the stamens turn upward; next, yellow pollen develops on the anthers; and then, the style lengthens and its tip turns upward. Pollinators come to sip the nectar gathered in the base of the flower, bringing pollen on their abdomen, which they rub onto the reflexed three-lobed stigma. The plant grows in clearances among subalpine forests. The flowering stems reach 20–40 cm tall. Linear leaves overlap at the base of the stems. The 3- to 4-cm-long flowers are pale purple. 23 June 1989, NE of Junbesi, Solu, alt. 3400 m, E Nepal

Polygonatum hookeri Baker   Convallariaceae

(Upper photograph) Flowers of this dwarf species may open before its seven to ten lanceolate leaves appear. A deeply buried rootstock sometimes produces a stem to 5 cm tall. The flower, which arises out of the axil of the lowest leaf, has a 1-cm tube and is 1.5 cm in diameter. 19 June 1992, NE of Mt. Masang Kang, alt. 4500 m, N Bhutan

Roscoea auriculata K. Schumann   Zingiberaceae

(Lower photograph) Forming colonies in grassy patches of evergreen forests, this species differs from *Roscoea purpurea* in having auricle bases on all leaves. It is 15–30 cm tall with linear-lanceolate leaves 5–20 cm long. The flowers are 5 cm across and usually pink. 13 June 1989, W of Lamjura Bhanjyang, Solu, alt. 2600 m, E Nepal

Iris kemaonensis D. Don ex Royale Iridaceae

I found this dwarf iris with large flowers, 6–8 cm across, on wet ground among willow and birch shrubs, which were still winter dormant and grayish brown in color. It bloomed just after snow melt. At the time of blooming, the leaves are normally only a little taller than the flowers. The drooping falls have beards of white hairs with orange tips in a line down their centers. Deep purple elliptical spots radiate around the beard. When I was photographing the flowers, a bumblebee landed on a fall, crept ahead into a gap between white hairs and a style lobe, then came out, smeared with yellow pollen on the back. 22 May 1989, SW of Mt. Manaslu, alt. 3700 m, C Nepal

Cypripedium cordigerum D. Don   Orchidaceae

Growing in oak and hemlock forests and seemingly protected by thorny barberries, this large lady's slipper orchid reaches heights of 25–60 cm. The alternate, ovate leaves are 10–15 cm long and enfold the flowering stem at its base. Both the sepals on the top and bottom and the petals on the left and right are pale green and 3–4 cm long. There is a white pouch-shaped lip where the side petals come together. The pouch is occasionally marked with pale brown blotches. Leeches lurking under the leaves of *Anemone obtusiloba* and *Fragaria nubicola* tried to climb onto my boots as I took this photograph. 11 June 1991, E of Dhorpatan, alt. 3000 m, W Nepal

Cypripedium tibeticum King ex Rolfe   Orchidaceae

On alpine pastures in strong sunshine and dry wind, the flower appears atop a young stem that is yet enfolded by young leaves and sometimes curved to suspend the heavy flower with its bag-shaped lip laid on the ground. In shaded forest edges, as in this photo, the flower appears with developed stem and leaves, and is more vivid in shape and color.

The plant measures 10–25 cm tall. Larger leaves are ovate to elliptic, 6–10 cm long. The flowers are solitary, dark purple to maroon, with yellow-green striations among parallel veins on sepals and petals. The lip projects forward with a wide circular mouth. 16 June 1992, W of Laya, alt. 4000 m, N Bhutan

Pleione hookeriana (Lindl.) J. Moore   Orchidaceae

No other Himalayan epiphytic orchid grows higher than this pleione, which can be found as high as 3700 m. It grows on mossy trunks and banks among hemlocks, tree rhododendrons, and oaks. The pseudobulbs, less than 2 cm long, nestle under thick layers of moss where they are able to store up sufficient nutrients to produce a plant 7–12 cm tall. The single flower stem and leaf arise simultaneously from that base. The elliptic leaf is 5–7 cm long with impressed parallel veining. Measuring 4–6 cm across, the pink flower, sometimes white in dark forests, has orange-red blotches on the lip. 13 June 1989, E of Lamjura Bhanjyang, Solu, alt. 2800 m, E Nepal

Ephedra pachyclada Boiss.   Ephedraceae

This plant grows in dry stony ground in the Himalaya and can reach 1 m tall. At higher elevations, as shown in the photo, it measures 5–15 cm. The green stems are 1 mm in diameter with opposing branches and 1- to 2-mm-long, brown, scalelike leaves at the nodes. The 7-mm-long reddish, ovoid fruits project from the nodes, consisting of solitary flattened black seeds covered with two or three sets of succulent red scales. Goats and sheep devour the branches, which contain ephedrine, a well-known stimulant and medication for asthma. The white foliage in the background is one of the dry-land artemisias. 31 July 1993, near Shaigiri, S of Mt. Nanga Parbat, alt. 4000 m, N Pakistan

Conversion Chart

3 mm = ⅛ inch	3100 m = 10,230 feet
6 mm = ¼ inch	3200 m = 10,560 feet
10 mm = ⅜ inch	3300 m = 10,890 feet
	3400 m = 11,220 feet
1 cm = ⅜ inch	3500 m = 11,550 feet
2 cm = ¾ inch	3600 m = 11,880 feet
3 cm = 1¼ inches	3700 m = 12,210 feet
4 cm = 1½ inches	3800 m = 12,540 feet
5 cm = 2 inches	3900 m = 12,870 feet
6 cm = 2¼ inches	4000 m = 13,200 feet
7 cm = 2¾ inches	4100 m = 13,530 feet
8 cm = 3 inches	4200 m = 13,860 feet
9 cm = 3½ inches	4300 m = 14,190 feet
10 cm = 4 inches	4400 m = 14,520 feet
	4500 m = 14,850 feet
50 m = 165 feet	4600 m = 15,180 feet
100 m = 330 feet	4700 m = 15,510 feet
2600 m = 8580 feet	4800 m = 15,840 feet
2700 m = 8910 feet	4900 m = 16,170 feet
2800 m = 9240 feet	5000 m = 16,500 feet
2900 m = 9570 feet	5100 m = 16,830 feet
3000 m = 9900 feet	5200 m = 17,160 feet

Bibliography

Cribb, P. 1997. *The Genus Cypripedium.* Portland, Oregon: Timber Press.

Davidian, H. H. 1982–1995. *The Rhododendron Species.* 4 vols. Portland, Oregon: Timber Press.

Fletcher, H. R. 1975. *A Quest of Flowers: the Plant Explorations of Frank Ludlow and George Sherriff.* Edinburgh: Edinburgh University Press.

Grey-Wilson, C. 2000. *Poppies: the Poppy Family in the Wild and in Cultivation.* Rev. ed. Portland, Oregon: Timber Press.

Halda, J. J. 1992. *The Genus Primula: in Cultivation and the Wild.* Englewood, Colorado: Tethys Books.

Halda, J. J. 1996. *The Genus Gentiana.* Dobré, Czech Republic: SEN.

Hara, H., ed. 1966. *The Flora of Eastern Himalaya.* Tokyo: University of Tokyo.

Hara, H., ed. 1968. *Photo-Album of Plants of Eastern Himalaya.* Tokyo: Inoue Book.

Hara, H., ed. 1971. *Flora of Eastern Himalaya: Second Report.* Tokyo: University of Tokyo Press.

Hara, H., et al. 1963. *Spring Flora of Sikkim Himalaya.* Osaka, Japan: Hoikusha Publishing.

Hara, H., et al. 1978–1982. *An Enumeration of the Flowering Plants of Nepal.* 3 vols. London: Trustees of the British Museum (Natural History).

Hooker, J. D. 1855. *Himalayan Journals.* London: John Murray.

Hooker, J. D. 1872–1897. *The Flora of British India.* 7 vols. London: L. Reeve.

Kihara, H., ed. 1955. *Fauna and Flora of Nepal Himalaya.* Kyoto, Japan: Kyoto University.

Lancaster, R. 1981. *Plant Hunting in Nepal.* New Delhi: Vikas Publishing House.

Long, D. G., et al. 1983–2000. *Flora of Bhutan.* vol. 1 part 1–3, vol. 2 part 1–2, vol. 3 part 1–2. Edinburgh: Royal Botanic Garden, Edinburgh.

Mierow, D., and T. B. Shrestha. 1987. *Himalayan Flowers and Trees.* Kathmandu: Sahayogi Press.

Nakao, S. 1964. *Living Himalayan Flowers.* Tokyo: Mainichi Newspapers.

Nakao, S., and K. Nishioka. 1984. *Flowers of Bhutan.* Tokyo: Asahi Simbun Publishing.

Ohba, H., ed. 1988–1999. *The Himalayan Plants.* 3 vols. Tokyo: University of Tokyo Press.

Ohashi, H., ed. 1975. *Flora of Eastern Himalaya: Third Report.* Tokyo: University of Tokyo Press.

Polunin, O., and A. Stainton. 1984. *Flowers of the Himalaya.* New Delhi: Oxford University Press.

Richards, J. 1993. *Primula.* Portland, Oregon: Timber Press.

Smith, G., and D. Lowe. 1997. *The Genus Androsace.* Pershore, England: AGS Publications.

Smythe, F. S. 1938. *The Valley of Flowers.* London: Hodder and Stoughton.

Stainton, A. 1972. *Forest of Nepal.* New York: Hafner Publishing.

Stainton, A. 1988. *Flowers of the Himalaya: a Supplement.* Delhi: Oxford University Press.

Storrs, A., and J. Storrs. 1984. *Discovering Trees in Nepal and the Himalayas.* Kathmandu: Sahayogi Press.

Taylor, G. 1934. *An Account of the Genus Meconopsis.* London: New Flora and Silva.

Wu, C. Y., ed. 1983–1987. *Flora Xizangica.* 5 vols. Beijing: Science Press.

Index of Botanical Names